This book belongs to

_____

For Cheryl Dickson, my sister.
Thanks for the laughs about practical jokes,
the songs while getting dishpan hands,
and the long-distance heart-to-hearts. I love you!

ONE TO GROW ON SERIES: MY BIBLE ANIMALS
Copyright © 1998 by The Zondervan Corporation
Text copyright © 1998 by Tracy Harrast

Scripture portions adapted from the HOLY BIBLE, NEW INTERNATIONAL
READER'S VERSION™.

Copyright © 1995, 1996, 1998 by International Bible Society.

Library of Congress Catalog Card Number: 97-61402

Published by Zondervan Publishing House
Grand Rapids, MI 49530, U.S.A.
http://www.zondervan.com
All rights reserved

Printed in China

98 99 00 01 02 03 04 /❖HK/ 12 11 10 9 8 7 6 5 4 3 2

One to Grow On™
Bible Series

My Bible Animals

Written by
Tracy Harrast

Illustrated by
Nancy Munger

ZondervanPublishingHouse
Grand Rapids, Michigan

Sheep and Their Shepherd

A shepherd takes care of his gentle lambs.
He names each of his fluffy sheep.
He leads and they follow him every day.
He watches them while they're asleep.

If one says, "Baa" and wanders away,
Could he forget it was lost? No, never!
Jesus said he's our good shepherd,
    And he wants us to be with
        him forever!

Sheep

[A shepherd] calls his own sheep by name and leads them out . . . His sheep follow him because they know his voice (John 10:2–4). *Suppose a man owns 100 sheep and one of them wanders away. Won't he leave the 99 sheep on the hills? Won't he go and look for the one that wandered off?* (Matthew 18:12).

Horses Say "Neigh"

If you ask a horse to come,
It will stomp its hooves and say, "Neigh."
You have to pull on its reins.
It shouldn't be stubborn that way.

When God asks us to listen,
We won't stomp our feet and say, "No."
Obeying God shows that we love him,
So we go where he wants us to go.

Horse

I will guide you and teach you the way you should go. I will give you good advice and watch over you. Don't be like the horse or the mule . . . They have to be controlled by bits and bridles. If they aren't, they won't come to you (Psalm 32:8–9).

The Talking Donkey

A man was riding a donkey,
But suddenly it stopped walking.
When the man said, "Giddy up"
—Surprise! It started talking!

An angel stood blocking the road
And kept the donkey from going.
Sometimes angels are near us,
Without us even knowing!

Donkey

The donkey saw the angel of the LORD. So it lay down under Balaam . . . He hit the donkey with his walking stick. Then the LORD opened the donkey's mouth. It said to Balaam . . . "Why did you hit me?" Then the LORD opened Balaam's eyes. He saw the angel of the LORD standing in the road . . . So Balaam bowed down . . . with his face to the ground (Numbers 22:27–28, 31).

Look at the Birds

Jesus said to look at the birds.
What a happy life they lead!
They don't try to grow their food;
God gives them all they need.

"You matter more than birds," he said.
So when you hear them sing in a tree,
Say, "God takes care of all those birds;
I'm sure he'll take care of me!"

Bird

Don't worry about your life and what you will eat or drink. And don't worry about your body and what you will wear . . . Look at the birds of the air. They don't plant or gather crops . . . But your Father who is in heaven feeds them. Aren't you worth much more than they are? (Matthew 6:25–26).

A Night With Lions

A king said people must pray to him
Or spend the night where lions stay.
E-v-e-r-y-o-n-e fears roaring lions,
So the king thought they all would obey.

Daniel did pray, but only to God.
He did what he knew was right.
So the king threw him into the lions' den.
But God kept him safe through the night.

Lion

[Some leaders said to King Darius,] "Don't let any of your people pray to any god or man except to you. If they do, throw them into the lions' den." Daniel did just as he had always done before ... He went to his room three times a day to pray to his God ... Daniel was brought out and thrown into the lions' den. [The next day Daniel told the king,] "My God sent his angel. And his angel shut the mouths of the lions. They haven't hurt me at all" (Daniel 6:6–7, 10, 16, 22).

A Fish
With a Surprise

Peter asked Jesus for help.
He had a bill to pay.
Jesus gave Peter the money
in a very unusual way.

Jesus said to catch a fish
And pull its mouth open wide.
Guess what Peter found?
A shiny coin was inside!

Fish

Jesus said to Peter, "Go to the lake and throw out your fishing line. Take the first fish you catch. Open its mouth. There you will find the exact coin you need. Take it and give it to them for my tax and yours" (Matthew 17:27).

Cows on Hills

Think of cows on a thousand hills.
Can you hear them all say, "Moo"?
God owns the cows on a thousand hills.
The world belongs to him too.

God is richer than anyone else;
He doesn't *need* money from banks.
But when we give some of it back to him,
It's a way to show him our thanks.

Cow

I don't need a bull from your barn. I don't need goats from your pens. Every animal in the forest already belongs to me. And so do the cattle on a thousand hills. Bring me thank offerings, because I am your God (Psalm 50:9–10, 14).

The Sneaky Snake

When we see a sneaky snake
  Wiggling and winding along,
    We can think of the Garden of Eden
    Where a snake told Eve to do wrong.

A hiss from a snake sounds like an **S**,
  That's the very first letter in "Ssssin."
When the devil tempts us, we say, "Go away!"
There's no way that he'll ever win!

Snake

*The L*ORD *God . . . said, "You can eat the fruit of any tree that is in the garden. But you must not eat the fruit of the tree of the knowledge of good and evil"* (Genesis 2:16–17). *The woman said, "The serpent tricked me. That's why I ate the fruit"* (Genesis 3:13). *When you are tempted, God will give you a way out so that you can stand up under it* (1 Corinthians 10:13).

The Pig Feeder

A runaway son was so hungry
As he fed oinking pigs in a pen,
That he almost ate their awful food.
But instead he went home again.

He worried his father wouldn't want him
Because he had been very bad.
But his father ran out and hugged him!
God loves and forgives like that dad.

Pig

The son wanted to fill his stomach with the food the pigs were eating. [He decided to go back to his father and say,] "I have sinned against heaven. And I have sinned against you. I am no longer fit to be called your son. Make me like one of your hired workers" ... While the son was still a long way off, his father saw him. He was filled with tender love for his son ... He threw his arms around him and kissed him (Luke 15:16, 18–20).

Too Many Frogs

Moses warned a king
To let God's people go,
Or too many frogs would come.
 But still the king said, "No!"

Because the king didn't listen
To the words that Moses had said,
"Ribbet, ribbet" filled the land,
And frogs hopped onto his bed!

Frog

If you refuse to let [my people] go, I will plague your whole country with frogs. The Nile River will be full of frogs. They will come up into your palace. You will have frogs in your bedroom and on your bed (Exodus 8:2–3).

Thirsty Deer

Deer love to run in the woods.
They get thirsty as they get hotter.
Soon it is time for a drink—
All they can think about is water!

Just as much as deer need water,
We need God in our lives each day.
We always feel the closest to him
When we read from our Bibles
and pray.

Deer

A deer longs for streams of water. God, I long for you in the same way (Psalm 42:1).

Smartie-Pants Ants

Have you ever seen a lazy ant?
None of them sleep life away.
Their six skinny legs go marching along.
They work very hard every day.

Ants plan and save whatever they get.
They're ready for what lies ahead.
We will get plenty of *our* work done, too,
If we don't snore all day in our bed!

Ant

You people who don't want to work, think about the ant! Consider its ways and be wise. It stores up its food in summer. It gathers its food at harvest time (Proverbs 6:6, 8).

A Hen Covers Her Chicks

A hen loves her chicks, so she
   hides them
Underneath her wings in a storm.
She's willing to suffer herself,
To keep her chicks safe and warm.

Jesus loves us just like that.
We're under his watchful care.
He helps us whenever we need him.
   When we run to him, he's
      always there.

Hen

Many times I have wanted to gather your people together. I have wanted to be like a hen who gathers her chicks under her wings (Matthew 23:37b).

Two by Two

Inside of Noah's big ark
God sent animals two by two.
Those that said, "Oink" and "Roar,"
Those that said, "Ribbet" and "Moo."

God kept them safe for 40 days
Till the rain and the lightning were done.
Here are some of those animals.
Can you name them just for fun?

Pairs of birds and pairs of all of the creatures that move along the ground came to Noah and entered the ark . . . For 40 days the flood kept coming. As the waters rose higher, they lifted the ark high above the earth. Every living thing on the earth was wiped out. But God showed concern for Noah. He also showed concern for all of the wild animals and livestock that were with Noah in the ark (Genesis 7:8–9, 17, 23; 8:1).

Author: Tracy Harrast
Illustrator: Nancy Munger
Project Management and Editorial: Catherine DeVries
Interior Design: Sue Vandenberg Koppenol
Art Direction and Cover Direction: Jody Langley